Count Me In

Count Me In

POEMS BY DARLENE YOUNG

Signature Books | 2024 | Salt Lake City

For Dad

a small girl and her father gaze at the stars

 Printed in the USA using paper from sustainably harvested sources.

Join our mail list at www.signaturebooks.com for details on events and related titles we think you'll enjoy.

Design by Jason Francis

FIRST EDITION | 2024

Paperback ISBN: 978-1-56085-474-6
Ebook ISBN: 978-1-56085-492-0

Contents

I.

2 The Baby That Became Me
4 Gethsemane at Age 5
5 The Fence
7 For Shame
9 Getting My Due
11 Motherhood
12 A Mother at Midnight
14 One Day You Finally Say Yes
15 Count Me In

II.

18 Moroni is Alone
19 Scrolling Through the Feed
20 Listening to Whale Song on the Internet
21 My Neighbors' Venmo Transactions
22 Hinge
23 Stiff-Necked
24 Memoir
25 It's Christ, That Wayne
26 My Son Asks for a Vocal Score of Handel's *Messiah* for Christmas
28 One of the Three Nephites Currently Serves in North America

III.

30 There Are Two Types of People in the World

32 "You're from Utah. You Must Be Mormon."

33 We Visit the Kirtland Temple, Now Owned and Staffed by a Different Church

34 What if I'd Not Been Raised to Know You?

35 You Are My Asymptote

36 What I Hope My Children Will Say on Mother's Day in 30 Years

38 Things I Have Pretended

40 The Words

IV.

42 Happiness in Winter

44 Hiding Up Treasures in the Earth Unto the Lord

45 Getting Up

46 Hope

48 Flies in the Back Yard

51 Suburb

52 The Middle School Band Concert

54 Morning

55 Cat, Before and After

56 Things I Have Lost

57 Toothpick

58 Even Psalm

V.

60 Undertone
61 To the Child Kicking the Back of My Seat at the Movie Theater
62 My Body in the Temple
63 Bumble and Gamble
64 My God
66 We Go Axe-throwing
68 Lazarus 2.0
69 Purchased
70 I Wanna Be God's Backup Singer
71 Notes
73 Acknowledgements

Not coincidentally, she sang.

—Jeanne Murray Walker

I.

Part of what you have to figure out in this life is,
Who would I be if I hadn't been frightened?

—Patricia Lockwood

The Baby That Became Me

sometimes it is necessary
to reteach a thing its loveliness
—Galway Kinnell

the baby that became me,
newborn, wearing the marks
of her recent move,
was beautiful

which had nothing to do with appearance

had never fallen
short, had never
fallen, had only
quirks not faults

as strange to guile
as an earthworm working its wormy ways

as worthy as tender lichen
and supernovae, knew skin and air and light
as kin (the same song only in different keys)

loved all equally, regardless of which side
of her skin it existed on
worthiness a word
without meaning

knew no reason
to look away, felt no call
to participate or
cause not to

had not yet met her lifelong bully—
her older self,
expected
to be adored, carried
no yesterday, accepted
all gifts

measured not
nor toiled
nor spun

Gethsemane at Age 5

In the movie, men with beards. Then a moment:
hands scratching at grass, curled and clawing.
Gasps. Violins.
Spikes and blood,
and that strange, t-shape
of a stick with a man on it.

It all swirls in her mind
with Santa Claus and Mr. Rogers
and the homeless man behind the library.

And—she doesn't know how she knows—
it also has to do with
that glimpse of Mama once,
kneeling bedside
beyond a half-closed door,
weeping,

and with the way
the stars in winter
blur when she stares at them, reminding her
of something long-ago
and familiar
she cannot name.

The Fence

Come over the fence, the neighbor-lady said.
My mother said, I'd better not—your dogs.
They're good dogs, the lady said. They don't bite.

I stood nearby, small. My mother—afraid of being bitten!
They were big dogs. But my mother was a big mother.

Come over, the lady said.
My mother said to me, stay here by the tree;
I'll just be a minute.

I stayed. My mother climbed the fence
into the lady's yard. The dogs yelped and jumped.
I heard them.

And then I heard my mother gasp.
Your dog, she said. Your dog bit me!
And the lady said, of course
he didn't. My dogs don't bite.

I couldn't see.

My mother said, he did! He just bit me! I need to—
I need to get these pants off.
She did not sound like my mother.

She remembered me then.
Go into the house, she said to me. I'll
be there in a few minutes.

In the house, I stood in the corner
behind the refrigerator. Later,
I would see the bloody pants
in the sink.

For years I would wake at night,
German Shepherds in my ears.
I hadn't known
mothers could sound small
and so far away.

For Shame

The story was told
among the older boys in my ward,
the "naughty" priests and teachers,
of a day one of them put vodka in the sacrament cups,
and how Sister Cutler had been the recipient,
scary Sister Cutler, the Relief Society president
with no sense of humor.

I, a good girl, was just old enough to know
that my shock was what the bragging boys sought,
and so I obliged, though I wasn't sure
whether it had really happened.
Though it was the kind of thing they would claim,
it seemed impossible—surely no one in my tight Mormon world
would even know how to get vodka. I was so sure

everyone I knew shared my values. For this reason
I once forced a little friend of mine
to pour out her cherry soda at the movie theater
because it came in a Coca-Cola cup
and therefore must be evil. Despite
her tears, I felt very righteous

until that evening
when her mother, whom I had never met,
phoned, asked to speak to me, and screamed
her rage, which of course I deserved, though
I didn't know then what I know now:
she and her daughter weren't even Mormon.

I stood with the phone pressed to my ear,
heart pounding—mortified, yes, but also
devastated at the betrayal of my mother,
who had taught me the evils of Coke,
and who had passed the phone to me without comment
having spoken to the woman,
having, surely, known what was coming.

Afterwards, she did not comfort me,
but went on with her work
as I sat weeping wretchedly in my first knowledge
that I could, in all innocent desire to be good,
make myself ridiculous.

And now I think of old Sister Cutler
and me as sisters, picture us
holding hands in the cause of innocence, of trust
in the orderliness of what turns out to be
a harsh and mocking world.

I could be wrong.
If the vodka thing really happened,
she likely sputtered a little, was annoyed,
made sure the bishop gave the boys the what-for,
but, being a mother of grown boys herself, maybe
later, eventually,
laughed it off.
I have raised boys myself now,
and I know that things happen, and that in a good community,
we laugh things off.
And in a good family, too.

But I won't laugh at everything.
A yearning woman sputters and spits.
A young girl weeps.

Getting My Due

I'm going to let my daughter read this so she knows how I felt!
—my journal, age 8, after a fight with my mother

That'll show her!
My daughter, I mean.
If I'd had a daughter.
That'll show me, showing her.

That'll show my mother,
the person I was really writing to
in all my noble rage—
my mother, who obviously
didn't understand me, meaning
I obviously didn't understand her,
never would,
because, surprise, surprise,
she was not long for the world.
That showed me!

Back then, at eight,
the biggest thing in the world was that I
be understood, meaning
get what I wanted, what
I was clearly entitled to.
The biggest thing in the world was I.

My mother understood, of course,
which I understand
now that I am a mother misunderstood
and sure of nothing.

What audacity, what wealth, at eight,
to have such an agenda:
the righting of all my deprivals.
Still sleeping with a nightlight
and yet such a warrior,
seeing out of the corner of my eye
the woman I might become,
and her powers.
Such fat, blind, gorgeous righteousness.

Dear daughter I never had—
guardian angel of my just deserts,
stand-in for the callous mother who,
it turns out,
was just tired—
forgive me for all I put on your shoulders.
I am so very tired.

Motherhood

when I was young
my mother was the sky
and I a small bird dark against her.
she left before I grew big enough
to see her clearly

so I thought that once you were born
I would be suddenly vested,
weighty enough to hold you and the world
in my orbit

Surprise!
once the world
became the world plus you
I awestruck shrank

the larger your need—
for teacher, defender, fixer
warrior—
the smaller I got

the bigger the job
the bigger the truck
the harder to reach the pedals

you fill my sky
sometimes I can't even see daylight
at your edges

at night I stare into the dark
and gasp for air

A Mother at Midnight

God
who knows
what I am
really like
will come and answer all.
I know
because my mother told me. Though
I didn't hear her until now.

That should be enough, I think. I think
too much.
Which is the problem. Thinking
it matters that I
prove to God that I
mean well when this is not about me.
Never was.

These days what I'm like,
even what I like,
is hard to know. My mother
told me once (when I wasn't listening),
it's enough to know God
made me.
Maybe so.

It doesn't matter,
God knows, how things look
if I can look, if I can like
what I can.

I'm older than my mother now,
so I should know
it doesn't matter
what I know.

She said so many things.
And I say so many things.
Let it go: my children
will know
what they know
when they know.

One Day You Finally Say Yes

After years of trying, wedging
straw into gaps, frosting

over the cracks

one morning enough
reveals itself as enough

you rub your eyes, open
your palms finally
to kit
and kitty meat
and bone ear
and earwig

your crows' feet, cobwebs in corners,
are lace, your body

a substantial claim dimpling space -time

satisfyingly .

so that grandbabies
and morning birds
and parking-lot kindnesses

succumb in their orbit

to your pull—

Count Me In

There are days when, visiting a depressed friend, I find
her houseplants are dying in the background
while she claims all is well
but also days when the morning percolates
in carnation pink glory behind and above
the smog, dewbangling the cobwebs.

Some days the smell of dirty snow, grim with the sins
of the city, makes everything taste of pity, mis-strung and trite,
but some days the sweet pale call of wind in spruces
summons me, though I'm not sure—don't even want to be sure—
what it's calling me to.

What a world, sodden with polkas and quick loans,
graffiti and gummy bears.
But the shook foil! The creek-cooled watermelon!
This grand, sad trunk-or-treat,
junk drawer of twist-ties and twine—
I still crave it, lick the back of the spoon.
The brindled shiver of a curtain in a drowsy afternoon,
bumblebees and Crackerjack, a toddler putting
his whole fist through the middle of his birthday cake:
enough! I'm snagged, in for the long haul
tap-dancing until the curtain call.

II.

Don't we all see
the lights of a city

from farther than we'd like?

—Adam O. Davis

Moroni is Alone

> *My father hath been slain in battle, and all my kinsfolk, and I have not friends nor whither to go; and how long the Lord will suffer that I may live I know not.*
> —Mormon 8:5

The smell of snow
is better than the smell of blood,
but still grim.

The gossip of wind up the mountainside,
a careful creek.
The ache of distant birds.

The sounds of battles long over
drift in shady paces. I put off
making new shoes.

There was a woman, once,
a hem disappearing in the haze.
My hair grows wild now.

On the back of my neck,
the breath of what I can't recall:

the sound of a child laughing,
the sense of the end of a workday,
the catching of a gaze.

Am I still here? A fox
passes nearby, looking
right through me.

Scrolling Through the Feed

Roll the dice. Lift a stone
and find honey, or earwigs
wincing in the glare. The drone
of faces flashing by like a zipper;
you risk getting snagged like thread
in the teeth of the world. Train
yourself to dip and go, kiss and sow.
Decide ahead of time: will you
speak or listen? Pant or mime?
Smoke and flags and kingdoms.
Each opening could be a trap-
door to the inquisition or a hitch
to winching someone's dark day
into the light. Hinge. Cast not
your pearls before swine, but leave
the windows vented.

Listening to Whale Song on the Internet

The opposite of checkbook and tumble-dry.

Stark liquid longing,   ancient as the stars,
    the sound of anywhere but here,
this fussy desk, this overheated room.

A call like traffic from the freeway on the edge of town
    when no one should be awake,
soundtrack for the walking of floors with a fevered child,
the sudden thought
that a marriage might be over. It sirens

to the young man trudging home
  from a sleety bus stop, the old man
heartsick for sleep.

Scientists included whale song on a recording
  launched into outer space, because what else
speaks so well of distance,   of whistling in the void?

Perhaps it is not longing at all but a strange
  hallelujah, or a clever whale joke to be passed
      through wet fathoms—
and so, for the rest of us, it is the sound of "lost in translation,"

"you had to be there." Missed
connections, dropped
    glances. What might have been.

The taunt of creatures who glide and soar,
  it strums on our yearnings, recalls dreams   of flight.
      A summons

to homesickness. My bones thrum
    as if to something familiar from too long ago—
maybe I recognize my own mother's voice   the way it sounded
when once I was curled
        in my own water-world.

My Neighbors' Venmo Transactions

Marco gets spray tans and Amy gets botox.
Lisa and Julie take Tammy for cake.
Bonnie pays someone named Henry for "muscle."
Apparently Georgia's long lashes are fake.

Now Julie and Tammy take Lisa for coffee.
Mari pays Tina, her daughter, for chores.
Tina, in turn, pays Samantha for highlights.
Rob's to Enrique involves football scores.

Now Tammy and Julie spend time getting facials—
(I'm hoping that Lisa, invited, just passed).
Georgia pays Sondra for something called "drumming,"
claiming it helped her sleep better at last.

I admit I'm a voyeur. These virtual windows
I peep through to spy on my neighbors and friends—
just a way to find out how to be someone different,
as if one could see truth through a digital lens.

Enrique pays Rob for "those sick wings at Tommy's."
Vi is mysterious—a goat and a nose?
Josh gets a Slurpee with Kimmy and Amy—
While Kim pays him back, Amy sends him a rose.

Hinge

Stacked knuckles of fate,
metal fortune cookie. Gate
or docket, ball-and-socket,
pat your pocket.
Maybe, if you're nice.
Maybe not. Fuzzy dice.
Fulcrum of due or die;
flip a coin, stew or try.
Knock, knock . . .
you're there.
Partly cloudy, blowing fair.
Bacon, beacon,
wake or weaken.
Dap to the guru, nod
at the shrine. Come on in—
the water's fine.
Raindrops on pavement,
cricket, frog,
plastic menu, breath, fog.
Gist and gesture,
kiss and measure.
Grass or gravel,
door or gavel.
Red scarf in a tree,
what happened, what could be.
If only, and—
probably.

Stiff-Necked

Caught in the drainpipe
of this tin-can quick-charge one-use world
I've had enough.
Blast me, Lord; tear the roof right off.
Crack me open
like a book spine puckered new; splay me.
Dog-ear me.

Breathe me; knead me. Tender me and tinder me,
hoard and toss and trundle me,
yea, even to and fro.

Enwrap, enrapt, and dandle me,
dangle, dash and shatter me.
Tethered, I will down-dog, belly high,
or down-shift. I will bow.

I will pour myself through your sieving fingers;
clarify me pure as rendered butter,
silken-smooth and mellow.
I would be honed
and owned.

Memoir
(after Vijay Seshadri)

The real story of a life is the story of its humiliations,
and mine jolt me from my 5 a.m. drowse
so that my hands fly to my face,
pillow-smashed and bleary,

and only the cat sees,
everyone else in the house dreaming
their own shames at that hour,
my personal God-reckoning hour,
the hour of flinch.

Once
I denied my guilt
in front of the one I'd betrayed,
both of us knowing I lied.

Once I ignored
the one I loved
to please the one I feared.

I habitually laughed too loud
at my own jokes, and, laughing,
opened my mouth too wide.

Once I said something cold
to someone already hurt.

At 5 a.m., the words I've said
circle like carrion-birds.
I grovel in the sheets like near-roadkill
scraping my way to the bushes
on the far side of the road.

It's Christ, That Wayne

But Christ is all, and in all.
—Colossians 3:11

It's Christ, that Wayne,
or Julie. Yea, and even Phil
of the empty coffeepot.

The check-out clerk,
clumsy-fisted. The man-
spreader on the subway,
snoring.

Not just the garbage man
but his screaming truck,
even the diaper left behind
in the grass. Behold.

Spam mail, twisted
headlines scrolling Las-Vegas-
style at the bottom of screens, shocked
emojis. Hearken!

Bow to all babies, all
bridges, everything
that pierces, oozes,
weeps. Holy
is all breath—

even sour, even
yours.

My Son Asks for a Vocal Score of Handel's *Messiah* for Christmas

After those rainboot years when you turned wide-eyed
anywhere I pointed came the years you shrank
from my hand, stared
out of car windows, refused
to let us take your picture.

All that time I was forgiving you,
mostly. All that time I was thinking of myself
at fourteen, my exasperated parents, and of the way people go
and come into themselves.
I knew my job: sit ringside,
resist expectation.

So now
your grins at anything I've pointed to
are like prizes in the Crackerjack,
a white-elephant gift that for once
holds the really good chocolate
instead of the itchy socks.

I invited you here, and so I play the hostess,
responsible for all you enjoy
and all you don't. I apologize.
For smog. Sorry. Mosquitos.
Sorry for violence and poverty, the flu,
awkward moments.
Modern politics. Sorry,

so very. But:
lilacs!
Sage in a balmy desert dusk!
And yes,
the thrill of nailing that intricate musical line
that crochets and crescendos,
culminates in a perfect Hallelujah!
And someday, maybe, a chance
to share it with your own child—
this breathless, spangled ride.

One of the Three Nephites Currently Serves in North America

The big things he can handle: tsunamis,
earthquakes, and, yes, even a pandemic
or two. Those things, he's trained for—tucking
the head and powering forward like a
running back; he can make the hard plays.
Besides, he loves how compensatory blessings
stream behind every major incident like seedlings
after forest fire, loves the way, in calamities,
God plays peek-a-boo with souls who'd forgotten
His face. No, it's the little things that weigh
on him. They niggle. Styrofoam peanuts,
Check-n-Loans. True, there are good things
about this first-world culture—in-sink disposals,
for example. Curbside grocery pick-up. And
his jazzed-up body is nice—no need for haircuts
or a gym membership. But lightbulbs still burn out,
and brake pads. There's global warming,
and late-night talk shows. So many hunched shoulders.
His retreats to the desert grow more frequent.
Everything blurs together, sometimes—the year
he spent driving a school bus, the three
changing diapers at an elderly nursing home.
Last year, the D.M.V. He begins to leave
sticky notes around the house to remind himself:
"Cheesy fries." "Hummingbirds." For every
cardboard sign near the on-ramp, there is a young boy
with hair in his eyes floating paper boats
in the gutter. "Middle-school tuba players,"
he writes. "Tailgate parties." "Meals on Wheels."

III.

after all this, still
one of us can't know another.

—Katie Ford

There Are Two Types of People in the World

I wish
I spoke moon.
—Bob Hicok

There are two types of people in the world:
those who can do the moonwalk and those who speak moon.
Fans of the Bee Gees and earners of BA's.
People who look out windows and people who look in.
Nail-chewers and whale-watchers.
Paper or plastic?

There are people who plant gardens
and people who have lain in dirt and sucked
the stems of grass.
People who count the cost and people who see angels.
Some people snore, while others snort, snarl, drool, and slur,
as appropriate and on demand.
The dainty and the stingy.
Chopsticks and stick shifts.

There are people who save the plums in the icebox
and those who run naked with sticky fingers, bees in their hair.
People who can spell *hors d'oerves* and people
who are too good for that.
Those who interrupt others, and those who
weren't even there.
Whistlers and whiners.
Liars and sighers.

There are two types of people:
those who wish to be cremated and scattered,
and those already flying in their dreams.
Those who can sing all of "Hey Jude," and those
who've memorized the Table of Elements.
Down-doggers and helium suckers.
Hand washers and wand wielders.
There are people who've licked flagpoles and people who've licked
the curled flower bud palms of newborns.
Lovers and wincers.
Sinners
and gone.

"You're from Utah. You Must Be Mormon."

The great and spacious building suddenly
is not that Lego monstrosity
you see in all the pictures, but this cruise ship,
and the people pointing from the roof
are not pointing from the roof at all
but sitting here around you slurping soup;
and, really, they're not pointing at you at all,
but just politely asking.
                                        It's your fear
that points at you instead. In fact these folks
don't even care. They've moved on. But here you are
babbling on, betraying your beliefs,
your ancestors, your culture that, in fact,
you really love,
                        by downplaying everything.
Yes, you are a Mormon but
not *that* kind of Mormon.
Yes, you are a stay-at-home mom
but not *that* kind of stay-at-home mom.
Yes you have a bunch of kids
but not *that* kind of barnyard family.
You talk too much. What can you say? You are
alien. Ridiculous to think you're not.

OK, so you believe in sin. And duty. And,
as you're sure they fear, you're trained to seek a chance to sell
a greater happiness if they could live like you. Supposedly.
Or something somewhat like that. In some way.
You shoulder the burden of this eternal self-
consciousness with the garment lines.
                                                Sweetheart,
order the mousse cake; relax. They're not asking at all;
they think of you, in fact, much less than you suspect.
Why don't you try
doing the same?

We Visit the Kirtland Temple, Now Owned and Staffed by a Different Church

The guide looks like she's seen some days, and they have made her kind.
Some in the group brush by her, won't meet her eyes.
She asks our newly-called missionary son to play the organ, and we all sing
"The Spirit of God Like a Fire is Burning," and my neck-hair rises.
This place. Strange, like all temples. A place of disjuncture,
of gaps, synapses for sparks to jump. A place of slippage.
I see that the guide feels it too. Where is her source,
her destination? Maybe she will be me, or was me once.
Maybe we'll merge in the middle in some new kind of place.
The difference between believing and wanting to
is a curtain in a breeze, a badly-timed sneeze,
a turned ankle where the baby spilled her juice. It's catching,
or not, something in the corner of your eye. Maybe a mote.
Fine print, mosquito wings, cilantro on the tongue.
Aware of my own hearing loss at higher decibels, I freely admit
there are things I'm missing. She and I believe
at different frequencies. On a spectrum, where do colors divide?
Stepping out of the building, we both blink in the sunlight.

What if I'd Not Been Raised to Know You?

I think I would have noticed. You call to me in pluckings
of strings in the dark, in salty seaweed and woodsmoke
and crickets and even the traffic. I would hear, I think.
I'd find you in my own breath, in the 3 a.m. street-
light on my pillow, the tug of a baby latched on my breast.
I'd feel you in the heartswell of a choir of others who seek you,
the skinny young Orthodox Jew I saw davening
in his car in the parking lot, the old man bowing over soup
at the diner. The teenage church boys pant as they shovel
the holy snow from the driveways of the widows on my street
making the din of Zion, the same song sung in AA meetings
or at Stonehenge and I am not tone deaf. I would turn
my head. I would have scented you on the wind.

You Are My Asymptote

Dear god of aardvarks and yard sales, drowned
kittens and Bernie mittens, be my valentine.
I near you, and near you again. You are the gnats
in the tent after I dim the lantern, humming
in my ears making me twitchy and wild. I am a child,
blind-man bluffing my way to you. God of the grit
and grind, the gaze and gawp, the garbage-
picking big-eyed racoon with fleas, you tease. You
who make meat sweet in the wilderness hover
on the horizon in a pillar of smoke so close I can smell
the singe in the air. I work towards you
like a beached whale melting into the sand, a hit deer
who can't rise gazing at the sky, the sky.

What I Hope My Children Will Say on Mother's Day in 30 Years

"She never complained."
—innumerable church talks, especially on Mother's Day

Not my mom.
When she was in pain, my mother mentioned it.
From this I learned that everyone hurts.

When she felt abused, she mentioned it.
From this I learned not to be silent.

When she doubted God, she mentioned it.
From this I learned that faith is what you do, not how you feel.

When she thought I was treating her unkindly, she mentioned it.
From this I learned I must be capable of behaving better.

When she needed more from me, she asked for it.
From this I learned I could step up.

When she saw something wrong, she mentioned it.
From this I learned how change comes about.

When she had too much work and was tired, she mentioned it.
From this I learned that adults struggle, too.

When she felt lonely, she mentioned it.
From this I learned that loneliness happens to everyone.

When she was disappointed in herself, she mentioned it.
From this I learned vulnerability.

After all this, I knew I could believe her.

When she spoke of moving forward in the face of everything,
I believed her.

When she said I was likeable,
I believed her.

When she said she loved me,
I felt its worth, coming, as it did,
from a real person.

When she spoke of joy in this life,
I believed her,

and when she spoke of grace, I believed that, too.
Verily, hers is a god I believe.

Things I Have Pretended

That I am not thinking about
the ketchup stain on my shirt right now.
That, when I bought the shirt, I could afford it
and deserved it.

That I've read that book, heard of
that band, know that politician and all
she stands for, remember the name
of the president of that country,
and what that word means. *(Nod, smile.)*

That your breath is fine,
and you've got nothing green
stuck between your teeth.

That I didn't eat that, and wouldn't care for dessert.
That this food looks good.

That I still believe in Santa Claus.
That I am Santa Claus. That I'm
grown up and therefore know what I'm doing.
That I am prepared.

That I feel better than this.

That I don't see you.
That my phone was off when you called.
That the thing you said last week didn't bother me.
That I heard you. *(Nod, smile.)*
That I didn't.

That I'm not yawning inside.

That I love someone, or
that I don't.

That I missed you. I didn't
miss you. That I like you. I like me.
I care what you think. I don't.
That I am not thinking about myself right now.

I am not terrified.

The Words

When I am worn
by trying for too long to fit into my life like the answer
to forty-nine across in a puzzle mostly blank
because I don't know soccer stars and European rivers,
I drag myself here, bearing my blunders
like bits of bone in my braids. Laden, empty,
bag lady. In the locker room
I strip myself like paint, paling to transparent,
the better to receive, beggar of crumbs. For
there is something here.

I am given words.
"Clean, every whit."
The woman whose face bends to mine
means it,
and I believe her. She knows.
I leave, bearing the words with me
in my cupped palms. I will take them and stitch them
into my skin where they will knit
with my cells, forge new DNA,
make me wholly
unrecognizable.

IV.

I will
never get over making everything
such a big deal.

—Ada Limon

Happiness in Winter

A big pink ceramic bowl of oatmeal,
with raisins and nuts. Not pudding.
The metaphor here is that fiber makes
for a better life.
There must be something to chew.
I'm not saying, Love, that you are the lumps
in the oatmeal. But you are sometimes the texture,
sometimes the milk. I'm saying
God gave me teeth, and something to use them on.
God gave me other protective features:
eyelids, an ample behind. Jazz hands. Happiness

is the deer tracks in the snow
around the dump. It is the bare trees
against the snow, arcing. Bare trees
are the teeth of the stale snow.

Today, happiness is the furnace clearing
its throat before its purr, and this is not symbolic.
Some things are just nice.
Like the way
our young son bent tenderly over the banana
slug we discovered in the forest that summer. Or,
on this dreary day,
the memory of it.

Spring will come,
a caricature of itself vamping around
this poem and every other in its baubles,
banjo, and feather boa, and the bare
trees will break out their jewelry and play
along. The thought of it
is an itch on the roof of my mouth I keep
tonguing. A long way off.

Oatmeal can get me through a morning,
a nap through the afternoon, and then, at evening,
you come sauntering in.
It's not that hearing the doorknob rattle
means "happily ever after,"
but, especially in winter,
it's a nice way to end a day,
and a poem.

Hiding Up Treasures in the Earth Unto the Lord

> *And it shall come to pass, saith the Lord of Hosts, yea, our great and true God, that whoso shall hide up treasures in the earth shall find them again no more, because of the great curse of the land, save he be a righteous man and shall hide it up unto the Lord.*
>
> —Helaman 13:18–20

There are things I'm eager to bury,
and things I'm not.
The mirror reveals cilantro in my teeth
after a day of talking to People Who Matter.
What matters? Lord, take it, this wilted speck,
heavy dignity. But I'll keep the kiss of cool
curtain of twilight in the desert—may I?
Take my teenager's lack of sleep
and now his cough that lingers,
but can I keep the freckles he hates?
The way he won't meet my eyes—that's yours.
And his bedroom. And his tardies.
But that joke he cracked—it's mine.
I was laughing hours later.
Phone calls I should have made. Dizzy spells
that make the doctor shrug.
The sloping porch. And how I wish
that the old incontinent cat
would die. Do I get to pick and choose?
Or is it our bargain that I bury everything?
The singing full out in a well-
balanced choir, the day I walked with my love
in milky twilight in Juneau? Dark chocolate
and the one bra that fits? Is it all
or nothing? Rope burn: my hands
open and close, open and close.
This hideous, beautiful life.

Getting Up

Today I woke
and went out into the world
and that was a triumph.
I suppose the world
woke and went out into me—
also a triumph, though
I don't know which of us is the hero.
There is the flute, and there is the breath.

There is motion,
and always the question
of whether to ride it.
It pushes against my thighs
so that I have to cut side-wise
against the current
to get anywhere.

Where is there to get, or what?
What if I already got?
Up, I mean. I got up. There—
is that enough?
I should make a production
of it, dismount the bed,
throw my hands up like a gymnast:
Ta da! 9.9!

"To bear the burdens
that may be placed thereon."
Is it a promise or a threat?

What does failure look like
if not the not getting up?
Sometimes reaching the low-
hanging fruit takes everything.
I am a champion.

Hope

This story ends with me still rowing.
—Anne Sexton

In the kitchen, we've found
our way again to that stale-
cracker conversation, grooved

and grimed like these sticky
kitchen chairs, uneven, warped.

The trailing off of a voice,
muffled traffic through a window.
Dirty water glasses.

How did we get here?
Sometime years ago we dropped
the car keys in a snowbank
and never bothered to search,

figuring there would be a thaw. Now
our life is too often a dank
and sweaty waiting room
with only golf magazines.

I think of the back page
of my tax form booklet
that says *This page
intentionally left blank*,
lying through its teeth.

I leave the kitchen.
Truly blank
means there's still a chance, means
a place where God could write.

I lie down, splay myself
belly up, thinking
This page intentionally left blank.

I am Bethlehem, in a desert,
waiting. (As are you, back
in that kitchen.) Surely
something is coming.

Flies in the Back Yard

Behind my house is an area of space
where black flies
        of some mysterious type—fat, sluggish juicy things—
        love to congregate.
                They weave patterns in the air
                like Billy's lanyard,
        or an invisible maypole. Their swizzle-stick paths
        trace double helixes
in a column of curlicue
calligraphy.

Perhaps, like bees dancing the directions
to good flowers,
        these flies are performing
        a map for each other,
                pointing to a portal to a world
                of moonbeams,
        a place   a fly can rest in forever:
        fly paradise—or death—
which may be
the same thing.

Or they are creating a happening—
performance artists,
        tiny fly mimes patting out walls
        and peeking around,
                while the other flies, the fly audience,
                sit invisible to us
        in the catalpa.

Maybe they are stoned
or sugar-buzzed
from the fermenting berries
across the yard. Maybe
they are fly belly-dancers,
acting out for their fellow females
the process
of generating life, teaching femininity
in their ripple and flow.

Or break-dancers, teenage punks
on the fly-equivalent
of a run-down corner,
killing time, showing off,
preening for the chicks.

I used to try to dispel them
with fly traps or sprays,
used to daydream about giant nets—
they seem so dense and scoop-able—
but they came back. Or, rather, their older brothers
came back, sleeves rolled, cigaretted, looking
for someone they could make pay.

Or it was the B-company,
understudies
getting their big chance,
glamping and joyous.

These days I prefer
to consider it a performance
meant for me.
I pretend it's my own installment,
like a "water feature,"
lending ambiance.
There must be something holy and magnetic
about the particular spot of the earth's crust
above which they gambol and swirl:
fly church.
I no longer fear but hope that they know something I don't
about the potential and the magic
of a suburban back yard.

Suburb

The garbage truck broke branches from my tree,
now strung about the yard like butchery.
Such fractured paradise a suburb is.

It may be blasphemy, this line of trees
along my concrete curb. But sheepishly
I love it. I admit my lavish wealth,

these quiet evenings, sprinklers coming on.
The people wave, garage doors opening.
I'm smitten with it all. My wild love may be

obscene, when so much in the world is wrong.
Desperation, poverty, loneliness, blah, blah blah,
some of it very specific, and very specifically

behind a few of these same garage doors.
But God takes all forms, abides, and I
will greet him as I meet him, even here.

Don't tell me that's not him I hear
in my teenage neighbor's garage band
or in the sewage system that still works

despite the county politics: I know
a miracle when I encounter one.
I'll worship here with barbecue and rake,

in dumpsters at my curb and PTA.
I wave back to my neighbors from my porch,
refusing guilt. God bids me love. I do.

The Middle School Band Concert

An assemblage of characters, caught
at the age of caricature: trace
in their faces at once the chubby
children they were, the future
underslept bill-payers and clock-watchers.
Acne, orthodontia, the blousy orchid
of amateur eyeliner, the gelled hair of hope.

The boy with the huge nose
whose pants are too short
has the solo; we all cheer for him,
his grandparents the loudest.

Some parents
take turns in the aisles with cameras;
others stay in their seats
and text. Little siblings slide down laps,
creep along aisles.

The slouching girl at the vibraphone,
wearing a suitcoat and tie, and the girl
with the impossible posture at the piano.

All the faces—
think "petals on a wet, black bough"—
too tender for this world.

Can you see the future dot-com bigshot
in the gangly boy with the cymbals,
all Adam's apple and shag?
The lone female sax player
will become a housewife
and surprise herself by loving it.

One trombonist wears a fedora, cocked
over an eye, and the beautiful, sad
girl with the French horn
has left her body.

Heads bob to the count.
A group of athletes in the audience
yell the name of one of their own,
who ducks and blushes.

The sweat-stained, overworked conductor
in a shabby tie, everyone's favorite teacher
with his puns, knock-knock jokes
and nicknames, has forgotten, for the moment
the precarious potato peel trudge
of diminishing budgets and teenage
souls seeking redemption in the joy
of the music. Radiant,
he gets the longest ovation
from his students, at the end,
six of whom—
the ones whose parents didn't come—
walk him to his junky car
after helping him
turn out the lights.

Morning

A melancholy pale-blue poem about a man
and a tree in a field at dusk, deeply
symbolic, isn't this one. This one
is about a woman, kind of pudgy, and her
suburban back yard, and, yes, a tree,
and her cat. And the yard isn't beautiful,
and neither is the cat. Or the woman,
for that matter. But in the early mornings
before the commuter traffic coughs up,
the cat lifts his head from the bed
and birds in the tree chitter and call
as if they were anywhere, and the woman,
without opening her eyes, turns
towards the window, her hand on the cat,
and feels herself part of the tree, the call,
the yellow morning, even here
in this nondescript suburb, which is, she knows
actually, a pretty good place, as holy as any.

Cat, Before and After

I.

Tongue and twang, needle-barbed, felted,
he presides. Need is a word he would never consider—
he *allows* your service. Curling at the edges of rooms,
all fringe and frolic, sneak and sass, he slinks.
His tail ticks his dreams—of moths, the sharp-
angled scent of the plant he loves to gnaw, a full bowl.
Grass-tickler, discover of hidey-holes, taut
as a notched-arrow, twine-tense for the pluck-launch
bird-ward. Or flocked and puddled with abandon,
sopping sun. Slither and tine, he is lap-loller,
stretcher of time and tendon.
The smallest whisker-flick of sound vellicates his ears;
a familiar voice can talk them down. Everything
and nothing behind his stare, he's there
and back again unlooked for, on his own terms.

II.

It's spitting snow. I look towards the glass door
and find no solemn patient silhouette.
When I forced him into the carrier yesterday
for the leaden one-way trip to the vet, he struggled,
weakly, but made no sound. A dying cat
has no place in a poem. I will not
anthropomorphize his last hours. He was not
saying goodbye, nor "I forgive you,"
not reliving old memories. Hiding
under blankets, he wasn't seeking
a dignified exit—he simply wanted us
to quit bothering him. I'm left
with my glaring human need to be needed.
The truth: he lived alone, occasionally
allowing us into his dreams. Unclear
which of us haunted the other.

Things I Have Lost

A remarkably good deal on a used car. Two or three
umbrellas. Very few buttons.

Words, more and more each year. A credit card.
On a hot summer day in 1980, a *Space Invaders* competition
on the Johnson's Atari, but not by much.

Names—of books, of people, of the street we lived on for a few months,
but not my childhood phone number.
Toothpicks. Too many cats.
My mother's hair, and then
my mother.

An investment opportunity. Muscle tone. Too many contests
to count. My temper. A sweet moment with my teenager—
yes, but also my breath
from the ones I have caught with him, climactic
and unforeseen.

My place in the song when I had a solo in high school,
and, subsequently, my face, and then my nerve.
Manifold and various screen names and passwords.
So much sleep.

My hearing, in part, and so also the thread
of many conversations. Bookmarks. My respect
for most politicians but not my faith
in people in general, or their ability to change.
An entire poem in 2004.

Some battles, but so far not the war.
Some inhibitions. Most ambitions,
but not hope.
My dignity, over and over.
Count,
and the need for it.

Toothpick

Let us praise the toothpick,
small soldier, pokestick of the stuck,
lint-tickler, feeling its way. Sidekick
of popcorn stickle and poppy seeds
in the corner pocket, scrap-junk
until you really need it, the universe
screaming to a stop on a pistachio speck.
What is the polite way to use it—
behind a hand, looking away? You can tell
what kind of restaurant you're in by whether
and how it's available. Spelunker of particles
in eighth-grade braces, unclogger of sprinkers.
Gluemixer. Beats an unbent paperclip
for cleaning fingernails, clogged cheese graters,
nooks in the dashboard. Add mini-marshmallows:
presto! cub-scout tinkertoys, log cabins, slingshots.
Pocket-sized pick-axe, pithkit, pitchfork
of the prickle, splinter-rake. Pee-wee spork
of hors d'oerves. A stack makes good kindling.
Fantasize: two could prop open tired eyes
during a boring lecture. Trapped in the corner
of a junk drawer, it is the least of things. A mote,
a sliver split from a beam, a thorn,
a fragment split from something big,
like the moment everything changed,
like a momentous wink.

Even Psalm

Smog today, but I saw your wink in the pink
light of the peaks above it, heard your chuckle
in the plumes of trumpets and under-the-skin
drums of the high school marching band
practicing four blocks away. I felt you
at church yesterday in the glittering silent air
after the last notes of the organ solo, that
silent tolling wind that unfurled in the curls
of even old snoring Sister Bea, carbonating
our blood so that even the teenagers
glanced up from their phones, all of us
clanging, goose-bumped, rapped. Evening,
I sense you, nappy and wild, dancing
in the cat's yawn, the cut grass and the moths
lantern-drunk at the window screen. Holy
jack-in-the-box, strewer of breadcrumbs:
when I catch sight of your hem, for a time
I fear no evil.

V.

Have you finally stopped
shoulding all over yourself?

—Solmaz Sharif

Undertone

Evening comes on.
A woman raises her hand to the sky;
clouds are passing, but no plane. If it did,
people on the plane would look down
and see only a field. Buildings. Not the woman.
Not the boy standing at a chain-link fence
shuffling his feet, nor the Barbie in the gutter.
Somewhere, a dog drinks from cupped palms.
A woman takes a thimble from a basket, dips
her face down into her work like falling water.
I am in love with the loneliness of dusk.
Dusk is a paperback that's fallen behind the couch,
a handwritten grocery list tucked in the library book
by the reader before, that mysterious shadow who shares
your taste in reading, who probably stands half-
dressed looking at the trees dark against the snow.
The afternoon puts on twilight
like a woman donning stockings.
I need hold no longer to my skin.

To the Child Kicking the Back of My Seat at the Movie Theater

Apparently,
the world,
which arranges itself daily fresh
just for you,

is for kicking.

Just as noses are
for picking; flowers, too—
and dogs are for petting,
or fearing, or
bringing home.

Your feet in my back are
the world
coming at me in polaroid—
zip, out of the slot wet and vague,
and I won't know what was there
until later.

Here in front of you, I am
the lady of unfathomable age,
invisible,
in awe at your rhythmic insistence
at existence;

you are a universe.
All around me, universes in the dark.

Much has been lost.
Much will be.

My Body in the Temple

Halfway through the session, I become aware
of a full bladder and nothing else.
All that is holy is eclipsed
by flesh. I pant in claustrophobia
between the lady who snores
and the gum-chomper, suddenly surrounded
by bodies. I remember how,
during my last pregnancy, the gurgle of stomachs,
the smell of the chicken-a-la-king breath around me,
the man clearing his nose into his throat,
sickened me to such devilish and frantic irritation
I had to go on temple hiatus.
Sometimes the body is too heavy.

Like now—my bladder, an overripe melon,
makes it hard to stand and suck in to allow
the matron to pass me in the aisle.
Counting minutes, counting stages
in the ceremony, I pray an apology
to the woman whose name is folded
in my pocket. An ordinance requires a body,
I tell her. This is what you get.

When it's over—when I've changed clothes
with sloppy rush and found the bathroom,
I emerge so much lighter that this place
feels suddenly airy and bright. I love
this liminal circus, this foyer of glory
smelling of polyester, so earnest,
so strange. On my way out,
I take my time, stepping tenderly around
a bright spirit in an awkward old body
kneeling to tie her sister's shoes.

Bumble and Gamble

I said something wrong, and now
I'm shrunken like a kid hugging the wall
at the middle-school dance, scent of bad
burritos and sawdust. Lord, gather me

as a hen gathereth her chicks. There is
global warming and Coronavirus. Wars,
and rumors of wars. There are drunk
drivers, and I have to let my teenager

drive my car. The wind picks up.
A growing mole on my shoulder is the wind,
and I will sway and bend with it, and not see
the broken trees nearby. Swaddle me.

So many people try to disappear (yoga,
drumdances, pot), but I think it's you
they're looking for. Come out, come out
wherever you are. My porch light is still on

because my teenager didn't come home
last night. There are bills to pay.
These are your cues: *Marco*? . . . ?

Maybe that is you in the finches I heard chuckling
when I switched off that porch light this morning.
Or in the Walmart greeter in his wheelchair,
whistling.

I'm going with yes.
I'm betting it all on you,
hoping for the Daily Double.

My God

nothing anyone will read tonight
is wild enough
—Judith Kerman

I will fear no evil, for my God will not be contained.
Yea, and notwithstanding the violence of staplers,
the menace of chain-link, he flirts in paisley
and houndstooth, sneezes in patterns of Fibonacci.

All a dazzle dance in candy sprinkles and polkadots,
my God is a god of gluten and of the sideways glance.
He encompasses split ends and newsfeeds,
lost socks and doorbells. Yea, even infomercials—
even motels.

My God is a god of webby plastic in the landfill
and spinning wheels in the blizzard.
Grits and bootcamp, line-dancing and carpools.
Fake news.
Sun flares.

Found in the press of a hand, grand misunderstandings,
missed curfews, curt nods, curtain rods, and in the sinking sight
of blue and red lights in the rearview,
my God appears in unanswered texts, takeout,
toilet paper and twine. The dearest cat videos,
fuzzy dice. Hiccups, chants, wheezes and winks.
Juxtapositions, misapprehensions,
dizzy spells and earmuffs. He neglects not
parmesan cheese nor Parcheesi, paramecium nor peacocks.
Roaches, roadkill, roadrash, Raskolnikov.

Lo, He abides in righteous indignation,
right turns on red lights, lightning.
Bifocals and bleach, and the smell of it.
He abides.

My God is the god of running back into the house
for something forgotten, and of carseats
strapped backwards in minivans. Blessed
are the batteries, both dead and fresh.

Through bluster, blunder, and blush, I seek Him,
and I find.
Home free.

We Go Axe-throwing

I'm thinking *unnatural.*
Like eyebrow piercing, blue popsicles. But
some here wear plaid, conjuring woodsiness,
ruggedness. Think: solid men who walk on floating logs
and wrassle oxen. Nature as honorable foe.

But what is *natural* anyway, in a world of quirks
such as armadillos and preying mantises,
the cosmic migraine aura of the aurora borealis?
And every day a small animal naps on my lap,
vibrating her joy in a pleasant hum.
We've conquered nature,
evolving enough to breed something wild
to adore us.
Is that what God's bred in us?

That, and the ability to throw sharp weapons for fun
and high-five each other.
Social survival tied to the animal joy
of the resonant
violent
thwack.

I'm blind to its pleasure, taking no thrill
in competition. Also, I am terrible at it.

The employee tells me I am not assertive enough;
I have no follow-through.
"Picture something you're mad at," he says,
and I think: politics.
He adds, "At the bottom of your stroke,
imagine jazz hands." Violence and dance
in a warehouse that smells of beer and sneakers—as bleak
as a middle-aged woman's mustache, and I would know—

and yet, in the next lane,
a group of older women shriek,
and their husbands cheer,
and I don't know what they are all going home to,
but maybe the conversation in the car
will be hopeful, the news turned off.

Here, then, the real triumph of evolution:
a dusty, well-lit place, indoors:
a way to get through January.

Lazarus 2.0

Lazarus, who surely never dared
to lay his head
on a pillow
and close his eyes again.
—Laura Kasische

Wrong. At first, that's all he did—that, and staring at the wall. Then he took to wandering. Chasing the wind and the mist. Riding his motorcycle with no helmet. Eating undercooked lamb. (What was the worst that could happen?) He couldn't see right, his eyes seared with afterimage. He stopped children on the road, searching their faces. He lingered in rooms where people had died, asked to hold people's babies. He kept glimpsing things from the corners of his eyes. The words got stuck in his mouth, as if in a second language, as if overrun by some distant music. He gathered leaves. He turned towards birds like a homesick ghost.

Purchased

Ho, every one that thirsteth, come ye to the waters, and he that hath no money; come ye, buy, and eat; yea, come, buy wine and milk without money and without price.
—Isaiah 55:1

My hand is always reaching
for my purse, Lord,
digging among the Kleenex and lip balm for spare change.

But you, who've spared me, stare
at the grubby coins I offer up—
self-flagellation, martyr's trudge, deep sighs—

and smile fondly. *Silly girl.*

How I've got it wrong,
this contract between us.
You give me:
the universe,
sunlight in my kitchen,
peaches.
You ask of me:
a lifted chin,
open palms.

I would beg forgiveness for my pocket patting
but even that you've already given.

The only thing you refuse me at all
is the right to pay up,

knowing, as you do,
it would make me
just too grimly just
for heaven.

I Wanna Be God's Backup Singer

I'm not fightin' for the melody, Lord,
but could I back you up?
Just behind and to the left—
could I wear long white gloves and do a little pointing?
Big hair, big lashes, red, red lips—let me do-wop
shuffle, show a little leg. I'll take whatever part you need,
scarf-fluttering descant chime or the support underneath,
swingin' low and breathy in the dusk.
I can wail. I can arch
and dip, looking knowingly down off that stage so that
if someone happens to glance past the main act
I'll be there, sweet and solid as anybody's mama and lover
and favorite easy chair all in one, fleshy and worn just right
and a little surprising. Don't need center stage,
Lord, but let me strut with my sisters, in synch,
all swivel and sass. When you lift off, I wanna be
ridin' that jet stream coattail contrail conga line to glory,
rounding the bridge to one more chorus,
the one that brings us home.

NOTES

Epigraph, p. 5
From "After the Death Bed: Fourteen Lines Seperateld and Wandering," in *Pilgrim, You Find the Path By Walking* by Jeanne Murray Walker. Brewster, MA: Paraclete Press, 2019.

Epigraph, p. 6
From *Priestdaddy: A Memoir* by Patricia Lockwood. New York: Penguin, 2018.

"The Baby That Became Me"
Epigraph from "St. Francis and the Sow," in *A New Selected Poems* by Gallway Kinnell. Boston: Houghton Mifflin Harcourt, 2000.

Epigraph, p. 17
From "Index of Haunted Houses," in *Index of Haunted Houses* by Adam O. Davis. Louisville: Sarabande Books, 2020.

"Memoir"
Line taken from "Memoir," in *3 Sections* by Vijay Seshadri. St. Paul: Graywolf, 2013.

Epigraph, p. 28
From "Koi," in *Colosseum* by Katie Ford. St. Paul: Graywolf, 2008.

"There Are Two Types of People in the World"
Epigraph from "Elegy Owed," by Bob Hicok, in *Elegy Owed*, Port Townsend, WA: Copper Canyon Press, 2013.

Epigraph, p. 38
From "The Last Thing," in *The Carrying* by Ada Limon. Minneapolis: Milkweed, 2021.

"Hope"
Epigraph from "Rowing" in *Selected Poems of Anne Sexton* by Anne Sexton. Boston: Houghton Mifflin, 2000.

Epigraph, p. 53
From "Self Care," in *Customs* by Solmaz Sharif. St. Paul: Graywolf, 2022.

"My God"
Epigraph from "In Tornado Weather," by Judith Kerman, in *Poetry 180: A Turning Back to Poetry*, ed. Billy Collins. New York: Random House, 2003.

"Lazarus 2.0"
Epigraph from "Medical Dream," in *Space in Chains* by Laura Kasische. Port Townsend, WA: Copper Canyon Press, 2011.

ACKNOWLEDGEMENTS

These poems have appeared, some in a slightly different form, in the following publications. I'm grateful to their editors for giving these poems a first home.

"Cat, Before and After" *Thimble*
"Even Psalm" *BYU Studies*
"Happiness in Winter" *Poetry East*
"Hope" *Harpur Palate*
"I Wanna Be God's Back-up Singer" *Literature and Belief*
"Lazarus 2.0" *Literature and Belief*
"Memoir" *Clackamus Literary Review*
"My Body in the Temple" *Dialogue*
"One Day You Finally Say Yes" *Young Ravens Literary Review*
"One of the Three Nephites Currently Serves in North America" *WRKWNDR*
"Purchased" *Irreantum*
"Suburb" *Utah125*
"The Middle School Band Concert" *Poetry East*
"There Are Two Types of People in the World" *Poetry East*
"Undertone" *Exponent II*
"We Go Axe-Throwing" *Rathella Review*
"What If I'd Not Been Raised to Know You" *BYU Studies*